CW01676617

Contents

Scope and sequence

	Vocabulary	Grammar	Global Citizenship	Project
Welcome to The Rise and Shine Museum	**People and things in a museum:** app, camera, exhibition, museum, museum director, phone **Dates:** 1st–31st **Months:** January–December	We've got (cameras). We can (take photos). We like / don't like (science books). Do you like (football)? Yes, I do. / No, I don't.	**Appreciating history:** An article	A Museum Trail Card
1 Who are we?	**Features:** beard, big eyebrows, blonde, curly, straight, wavy (hair), freckles, moustache, ponytail, smile **Special things:** blanket, bracelet, coin, drum, earrings, necklace	What does she look like? She's got (curly hair). She hasn't got (a ponytail). What has he got? He's got (a drum). Has he got (a drum)? Yes, he has. / No, he hasn't.	**Special things:** always, never, often, sometimes	A poster about a friend
2 Let's use it again! **Review 1** All about us	**Everyday things:** bowl, box, cup, handbag, jacket, plate, pot, rug, shelf, sweater **Materials:** glass, metal, paper, plastic, rubber, wood	I like / don't like this / that (bowl). I like / don't like these / those (plates). Whose are these / those? They're mine / yours / his / hers.	**Upcycling:** huge, little, pretty, ugly	An exhibition of upcycled things
3 City of the future	**Places in a city:** art gallery, funfair, hotel, ice rink, market, restaurant, shopping centre, stadium, swimming pool, theatre **Activities:** go on a ride / shopping / to a restaurant, visit an exhibition, watch a match / a show	I like / love going to the (market) because it's (fun). I don't like going to the (theatre) because it's (boring). What do you like doing? Do you like (watching a show)? Yes, I do. / No, I don't.	**Appreciate your city:** boring, clean, dirty, lovely	A new city
4 Food for everyone! **Review 2** Our community	**Food:** apples, beans, flour, grapes, honey, lemons, pineapples, potatoes, rice, sugar **Containers and quantities:** bag, bottle, box, cup, glass, piece	There's some (rice) and a lot of (honey). There isn't any (bread). There are a lot of (potatoes) and some (pineapples). Are there any (apples)? Is there any (rice)? Yes, there is / are. No, there isn't / aren't.	**Not wasting food:** cakes, chips, lemonade, smoothie	A no-waste menu
5 Help our oceans!	**Sea animals:** crab, dolphin, jellyfish, octopus, seahorse, seal, shark, snail, starfish, whale **Care for the ocean:** clean the oceans, have a beach clean up, make a film, pick up rubbish, recycle rubbish, tell people	The sharks are (swimming). They aren't (jumping). What are they doing? They're (making a film). Are they (picking up rubbish)? Yes, they are. / No, they aren't.	**Our oceans:** brilliant, dangerous, safe, terrible	A play about helping the oceans
6 Let's play together! **Review 3** Our world	**Sports:** do athletics / gymnastics, go snowboarding / swimming, play badminton / baseball / basketball / hockey / table tennis / volleyball **Sporting activities:** bounce / hit / throw a ball, jump hurdles, run / win a race	I'm going to (play table tennis). I'm not going to (do gymnastics). What are you going to do? Are you going to (do gymnastics)? Yes, I am. / No, I'm not.	**Unusual sports:** badly, quickly, slowly, well	A sports weekend

Goodbye	**Goodbye from The Rise and Shine Museum**
Celebrations	**Museum Takeover Day, World Food Day, International Day of Forests, Museum Open Day**
Future skills	**Work with others, Respect others, Oral communication, Responsibility, Empathy, Being open-minded**

Pronunciation	
Unit 1 /k/, /g/	**Unit 4** /aʊ/, /ɪ/
Unit 2 /ʌ/, /ɑːr/	**Unit 5** /wəz/, /wɒz/
Unit 3 /juː/, /ɜːr/	**Unit 6** /θ/, /ð/

My Progress Chart

	Welcome	Unit 1	Unit 2	Unit 3	Unit 4	Unit 5	Unit 6
Listening	I can understand important information in short conversations.	I can understand questions and answers about people in my world.		I can understand important details in short conversations.		I can understand questions and answers in short conversations.	
Reading	I can read and understand some details in short texts.	I can identify specific information in a short story.		I can find and understand the details in short texts.		I can understand key information in short texts.	
Speaking	I can have a short conversation about my world.	I can describe the people in my world.		I can ask for and give information about my community.		I can ask and talk about future plans in my world.	
Writing	I can write a simple sentence to give information.	I can write an invitation to a party.		I can write a simple text message to a friend.		I can write a short letter to a friend.	

Welcome to The Rise and Shine Museum

1 museum director   2 museum   3 app
4 exhibition   5 phone   6 camera

Lesson 1

What can you see?

1 0.04 Listen and find.

2 0.05 Listen and point. Then listen and repeat.

3 Talk about the museum and the characters.

There's a museum director and her name is Eva.

What do you like to see at museums?

4 0.06 Listen and chant.

5 0.07 Listen and repeat. Then ask and answer.

When's your birthday?

It's on the 22nd of May.

I wonder... What can you do in a museum?

Song

It's the Rise and Shine Museum.
Come on! Let's explore!
It's the Rise and Shine Museum.
Exhibitions on every floor!

We've got tablets,
We've got the app,
We can go online,
We can use the map!

Chorus

We've got cameras,
We've got phones, too,
We can take photos,
We can make films, too!

Chorus

Lesson 2

1 0.09 Read and sing.

2 0.11 Listen and answer. *True* or *false*?

3 Make sentences about the picture.

Grammar

We've got cameras. We can take photos.

take photos | use the map | go online

I can shine!

4 What have you got? What can you do?

We've got pens. We can write stories!

I can talk about things we've got and actions we can do.

Lesson 3

1 0.12 **Listen, point and say. What things can you see in the story?**

1 

important photos

2 

special toys

3 

popular books

4 

fun games

2 0.13 **Listen or watch. What's inside the cupboard?**

3 **Read again and complete the sentences.**

1 Marco wants to put a… in the time capsule.

2 Sofia wants to put a… in the time capsule.

3 Sofia sees games and… in the very big room.

I can shine!

4 **Imagine you've got a time capsule. What do you want to put inside it?**

We can put some popular books inside the time capsule.

I can talk about things we can put inside a time capsule.

Rise and Shine Museum

1 0.14 Listen and say. Which books do all the children like?

a science books b storybooks

Look. Which things do you like? Which things don't you like?

2 0.15 Listen and read. Then chant.

Grammar builder

	science books.
We like	
	storybooks.
We don't like	
	museums.

I can shine!

3 Ask and answer.

Do you like football?

Yes, I do.

Me too! We both like football!

I can talk about things we like and don't like.

Lesson 5

1 Look and number.

2 Listen and read. Choose the best heading.

0.16

a Closing a time capsule

b Opening a time capsule

c Closing and opening a time capsule

3 Read and choose the correct answers.

1 There are *photos / computer games* and a newspaper inside the time capsule.

2 Tina is *opening / closing* the time capsule today.

3 The time capsule is *31 / 50* years old.

4 Miss Brown's first name is *Kate / Tina*.

1970, London

Hi! I'm Kate Brown. It's the 31st of August. Today is an exciting day! We're closing our class time capsule. There are some photos and today's newspaper inside!

Kate Brown, 1970

Today, London

Hi, my name is Tina. Today, it's the 1st of September. We're opening our class time capsule. It's 50 years old! Time capsules help us learn about the past. Our teacher, Miss Brown, is helping us.

There's an old newspaper inside. We can take it to the museum! There are also some old photos of the class. The children have got books, pens and pencils. We've got books, pens and pencils in our classroom, too!

Kate Brown, today

Look, Tina! Can you see that girl in the photo? That's me! This is my time capsule! I'm very happy to see it again!

Work in groups. Agree on two things to put inside your class time capsule.

I can shine!

4 Complete the sentence.

There are… and… inside our time capsule.

I can write about a time capsule.

Our Museum Trail Cards

Step 1 Review

1 Match. Then add more words.

fourth important photos exhibitions app toys museum director

museum *dates* *time capsule*

2 Look. Make sentences.

We've got	books. / cameras. / tablets.
We like	popular books! / important photos! / fun apps!
We can	read stories. / take photos. / use the app.

3 Do you and your friends like the same things?

Step 2 Create

4 Draw a time capsule on your Museum Trail Card.

5 Decide on one of the things to put inside your time capsules. Draw it on the cover.

We like cameras. We can put some important photos inside our time capsules!

Time to shine!

6 Present your Museum Trail Card to the class.

7 Which objects are popular in your class?

I can talk about a time capsule.

1 Who are we?

Rise and Shine **Museum**

- Ask and say what people look like.
- Talk about my special thing.
- Ask if I don't understand something.
- Write a description of a special thing.
- Talk about people and their special things.

I wonder... What's the most common eye colour in the world?

1 big eyebrows	2 curly hair	3 moustache	4 pony tail	5 beard
6 wavy hair	7 straight hair	8 smile	9 freckles	10 blonde hair

Lesson 1

What can you see?

1 1.01 Listen and find.

2 1.02 Listen and point. Then listen and repeat.

3 Watch and listen.

4 Look and say.

I've got straight, blonde hair. What about you?

He's got curly, black hair and a beard.

They've got blue eyes.

Song

We're all different!
We've got different names,
We're all different!
But we're all the same!

What does he look like,
That boy over there?
He hasn't got glasses,
He's got straight, black hair!

Chorus

What does she look like,
That girl over there?
She hasn't got freckles,
She's got curly, brown hair!

Chorus

What does he look like?
That man over there?
He hasn't got a beard,
He's got wavy, black hair!

Chorus

Lesson 2

1 1.03 Read and sing.

2 1.05 Listen, find and point.

3 Make sentences about people in the picture.

Grammar

What does he / she look like?

He's **got** straight, black hair and green eyes. He **hasn't got** freckles.

She's **got** curly, brown hair and brown eyes. She **hasn't got** a ponytail.

I can shine!

4 What does your family look like? Ask and answer.

mother father sister
brother aunt uncle
grandfather grandmother

What does your brother look like?

He's got curly, brown hair and brown eyes but he hasn't got a beard!

I can ask and answer about what people look like.

Lesson 3

1 1.07 Listen, point and say.

1

bracelet

2

necklace

3

earrings

4

drum

5

coin

6

blanket

2 Look. Which things can you see in the story?

3 1.08 Listen or watch. Then choose.

This exhibition is about special *people / things.*

Rise and Shine **Museum**

4 Read and answer. *True* or *false*?

1 Sofia hears a piano.
2 Hugo smells chocolate.
3 Eva's special thing is her necklace.
4 Eva can't find her special thing.
5 Socks helps the children find the bracelet.

I can shine!

5 What special thing do you want to put in the exhibition?

I want to put my… in the exhibition because… .

I can talk about my special thing.

Lesson 4

1 1.09 Listen. What's Zoe's favourite thing in the exhibition?

2 1.10 Listen and read. Then chant.

Grammar builder

What has he / she got?		*He / She's got a drum.*
		He / She's got a necklace.
Has he / she got	*a drum?*	*Yes, he / she has.*
	a bracelet?	*No, he / she hasn't.*

Ask and answer about the picture in Activity 1.

a necklace a blanket
blue eyes curly hair
blonde hair a ponytail
some photos a toy
a football

3 Choose a person. Then ask, answer and guess.

Has this person got curly, red hair? — *No, she hasn't.*

Has she got a necklace? — *Yes, she has.*

Is it Zoe? — *Yes, it is!*

Structures *What has he / she got? He / She's got (a drum).*

Lesson 5

1 Look. Describe the children and their special things.

2 1.11 Listen and read.

3 1.12 Listen again and repeat.

Pronunciation

4 1.13 Listen and say.

Can you see Gus the cat in the classroom there?
He's got clever, green eyes.
He's got curly, grey fur!

I can shine!

5 Describe a person. Then listen and draw. Ask if you don't understand something.

I can ask if I don't understand something.

Lesson 6

1 Look. Are these things special?

2 1.14 Listen, read and match.

1 My drum 2 My camera 3 My books

HOME | NEWS | KID REPORTER | SHARING | FUN TIMES

Special to me, important to everyone!

Tell us about your special things!

A ... are special to me! I love stories. This is my favourite book. It's about a pirate! He's got a red moustache and a long, curly beard! I think books are important to everyone. We can learn new things from books.

Ewa, 9, Russia

B ... is special to me! I ***never*** forget my camera when I go out! I take a lot of photos and I ***often*** make films of my friends. It's fun! I think cameras are important to everyone. They can take photos. They can also make films about special days.

Tom, 10, USA

C ... is special to me! I ***always*** play it on special days! I think music is important to everyone. ***Sometimes*** people play music when they're happy. They can play music when they're sad, too.

Gabriel, 9, Nigeria

Which thing in Activity 2 do you think is important to everyone?

3 Read again and choose.

1 Ewa lives in *Russia* / *the USA*.
2 She's got a favourite book about a *pirate* / *drum*.
3 Tom makes films of his *special days* / *friends*.
4 Gabriel plays *football* / *a drum* on special days.
5 People play *music* / *games* when they're happy or sad.

4 1.15 Listen. Which thing from Activity 2 don't they talk about?

5 1.16 Listen again. Complete the sentences.

coin cameras necklace books

1 Sara thinks that... are important to everyone.
2 Pierre thinks that... are important to everyone.
3 Sara's special thing is a... .
4 Pierre's special thing is a... .

Lesson 7

1 1.18 Listen and read. Then match.

This is my special thing. It's a small, old coin.
There's a picture of a man on it.
He's got long, curly hair and a moustache!
The coin is special to me. It's a present from my grandfather!
I think old coins are important to everyone.
We can learn about history from old coins.

1 The coin
2 The man
3 Old coins

a is small and old.
b can teach us about history.
c on the coin has got long hair.

Our writing workshop

2 1.19 Ideas generator Listen and number.

A

B

C

D

3 Give it a go Plan your description with a friend.

What's your special thing?
Describe it.
Why is it special to you?
Do you think it's important to everyone? Why? Why not?

I can shine!

4 Write a description of a special thing together.

I can write a description of a special thing.

My special people

Step 1 Review

1 Look. What do Kurt and Mia look like?
Are you the same or different?

hair eyes freckles eyebrows smile

Kurt	Mia

Kurt's got curly, brown hair. I've got curly, brown hair, too! We're the same!

Mia hasn't got freckles. I've got freckles. We're different!

2 Look again. What are Kurt and Mia's special things?
What's your special thing?

3 What can we say when we don't understand someone?

4 Is your special thing important to everyone?

5 Watch and listen.

My special thing is my camera. I think cameras are important to everyone because they can take photos of special days.

My special thing is my bracelet. Bracelets aren't important to everyone but this is special to me!

Step 2 Create

6 What does your friend look like? What's his / her special thing?

This is my friend… .
He's / She's got… .
He / She hasn't got… .
His / Her special thing is… .
We're the same / different because… .

7 Make a poster about your friend and his / her special thing. Are you the same or different?

8 Put all the posters together to create an *All About Us* exhibition.

Time to shine!

9 Present your friend to the class.

This is my friend Ben. He's got straight, brown hair and big, green eyes. We're the same because I've got brown hair, too. But Ben hasn't got freckles or a ponytail. His special thing is his favourite book!

10 What new facts do you know about your class?

I can talk about people in my class and their special things.

2 Let's use it again!

Rise and Shine Museum

- Talk about things that are near and far.
- Talk about using old things to make new things.
- Make and reply to invitations.
- Write an invitation to an upcycling party.
- Design and talk about upcycled things.

I wonder...
What can you do with old plastic boxes?

1 plate	2 bowl	3 cup	4 rug	5 sweater
6 handbag	7 pot	8 shelf	9 jacket	10 box

Lesson 1

What can you see?

1 2.01 Listen and find.

2 2.02 Listen and point. Then listen and repeat.

3 Watch and listen.

4 Look and say.

There are two red and white bowls.

What old things have you got? Can you use them again?

Song

We use our things again and again,
We don't throw them away!
We make our old things new again,
We do it every day!

Look at these cups!
Look at these plates!
Look at these bowls!
I think these are great!

Chorus

Look at those boxes!
Look at those pots!
Look at those sweaters!
I like those a lot!

Chorus

Lesson 2

1 2.03 Read and sing.

2 2.05 Listen, find and point.

3 Make sentences about the picture.

Grammar

I like **this** bowl. 	I don't like **that** bowl. 
I like **these** plates. 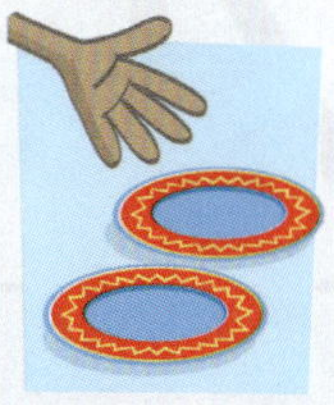	I don't like **those** plates. 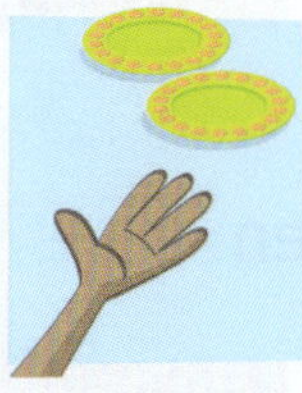

I can shine!

4 Talk about things in your classroom.

pen books pencil case
windows door
children tablets

Look at this pen and look at that book!

Look at these pencils and look at those pots!

I can talk about things that are near and far.

Lesson 3

1 2.08 Listen, point and say.

1

plastic

2

paper

3

wood

4

metal

5

rubber

6
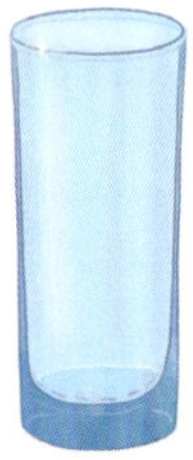
glass

2 Look at the story. Can you describe the things in the pictures?

3 2.09 Listen or watch.

What new thing do the children make?

4 Read again. Complete the sentences.

old shoes	rubber boot
plastic cups	old T-shirts

1 Gita uses... to make new rugs.

2 Zoe sees some... and some paper plates.

3 Marco finds some old clothes and some... .

4 Hugo uses a... to make a new flower pot.

I can shine!

5 Imagine you're at the exhibition.
What do you want to use?
What do you want to make?

I want to use this plastic cup. I want to make a new pencil pot.

I can talk about using old things to make new things.

Story value Understanding the importance of reusing things.

Lesson 4

1 2.11 **Listen and match.**

2 2.12 **Listen and read. Then chant.**

Grammar builder

Whose is	*this / that?*	*This / That is*	*mine / yours / his / hers.*
Whose are	*these / those?*	*These / Those are*	*mine / yours / his / hers.*

3 **Ask and answer about different things.**

Whose are these pencils?

These are mine.

Structures *Whose is / are this / these… ? This / These is / are mine / yours / his / hers.*

Lesson 5

1 Look. What are they doing?

2 2.13 Listen and read. When is the party?

3 2.14 Listen again and repeat.

Pronunciation

4 2.15 Listen and say.

I'd love to come to your party.
Parties are always fun!

But I can't come to your party.
Sorry but I can't come!

I can shine!

5 Invite your friends to some parties. Your friends answer.

Would you like to come to my upcycling party?

Yes, please. I'd love to!

No, thanks. Sorry, I can't.

I can make and reply to invitations.

Lesson 6

1 Look. Do you have these things in your city?

2 2.17 Listen, read and match.

A

B

C

Cool city upcycling

Things to do with the *ugly* rubbish in our cities

1 Box garden, Sydney, Australia

Many people have got old plastic boxes. In Sydney, there's a ***huge*** city garden. This garden uses plastic boxes! First, people grow plants inside ***little*** boxes. Then they put the plants into big boxes. They put these boxes together. The garden is very ***pretty*** and it's fun to visit!

2 Fish phone boxes, Tokyo, Japan

People don't use phone boxes now. In Japan, people put water in old phone boxes. Then they put fish in the phone boxes, too! Now, the phone boxes are interesting homes for fish! People love looking at the ***little*** fish. They take a lot of photos of the fish and the phone boxes!

3 Rubbish playground, Kathmandu, Nepal

People in Kathmandu upcycle ***ugly*** city rubbish. They use the rubbish to make an exciting playground! Children can climb and swing in this playground. Many people love the playground. It uses rubbish to make a fun place for children! Do you want to play there, too?

3 Read again and match.

before

1 old plastic boxes
2 old phone boxes
3 ugly rubbish

after

a an exciting playground
b a pretty garden
c interesting homes for fish

4 2.18 Listen and say. Where is the party?

a at the museum
b at home

5 2.19 Listen again. *True* or *false*?

1 Emin has some old plastic bowls at home.
2 Lisa has some old metal plates at home.
3 Everyone can bring some food to the party.

Lesson 7

1 2.21 Listen and read. Whose party is it? When is it?

Please come to my *upcycling* **party!**

To: *Ben*

From: *Lisa*

Where? *It's at my house.*

When? *It's on Saturday at two o'clock.*

Please bring some things for upcycling!

Our writing workshop

2 2.22 **Ideas generator** Listen, read and complete.

1 I've got these paper… and this huge… !

2 I've got some old clothes. Look at these ugly… and this old… !

3 I've got this old… and these plastic… .

3 **Give it a go** Plan your party with a friend.

Our upcycling party!

Where?

Which day?

What time?

Please bring:

I can shine!

4 Write an invitation to an upcycling party together.

I can write an invitation to an upcycling party.

My things and your things

Step 1 Review

1 Look and say the upcycled things.

This is a bowl.

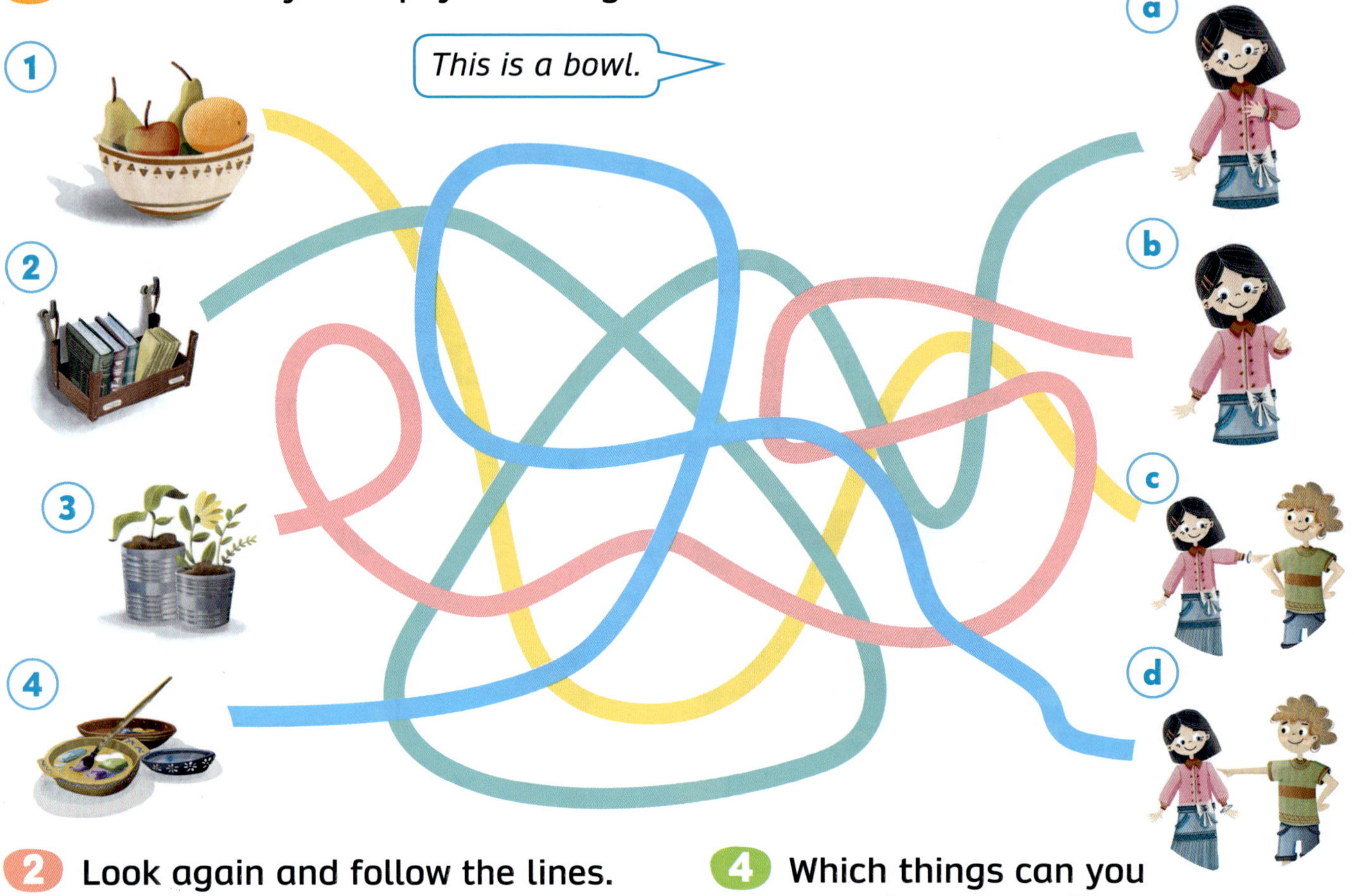

2 Look again and follow the lines. Ask and answer.

Whose is this?

This is his.

3 Invite your friend to an upcycling party.

Would you like… ?

Yes, please. I'd… . / No, sorry, I… .

4 Which things can you upcycle at home?

We can upcycle old cups and plates.

Yes, we can. We can upcycle…, too!

5 Watch and listen.

Step 2 Create

6 Look. Choose an old thing or things to upcycle.

7 Share your ideas about how you can upcycle your old things.

I can make a new pen pot from this old cup!

8 Design and talk about your upcycled things.

This is my new pen pot.

Time to shine!

9 Create a class exhibition of your new things! Ask and answer.

10 Which upcycled things are useful to you? Tell your friend.

I like these pretty bowls. Whose are these?

These are mine!

I can design and talk about upcycled things.

Review 1 All about us

1 Listen. What do the children want to put inside the time capsule?

2 Look. Ask and answer.

curly hair moustache blonde hair big eyebrows a big smile

What does he / she look like?

necklace bowl boxes flower pot dolls

Whose is this / that?

3 How can we use these things again?

4 Read. Who is Emma?

I'm Marco. I've got one sister. Her name is Emma. She's got straight, brown hair and brown eyes. She's got big eyebrows and a big smile. She hasn't got freckles. Her special thing is a bracelet. It's very old! It's a present from our grandmother.

5 Read again. *True* or *false*?

1 Emma's got curly hair.
2 She hasn't got big eyebrows.
3 She's got freckles.
4 Emma thinks her bracelet is special.

6 Write about someone in your family and their special thing.

MINI PROJECT

7 Create a class exhibition. Find things in your school bag. Look. Ask and answer.

Time to shine!

8 What you can see in the exhibitions? Complete your Museum Trail Card.

Museum Trail Card

1	I can read, write and talk about describing people and upcycling things.
2	I can ask and talk about what people look like and their things.
3	I can ask people to repeat something.
4	I can invite people to a party and reply to an invitation.

3 City of the future

Rise and Shine **Museum**

- Talk about where I like and don't like going in a city.
- Talk about activities I like and don't like doing in a city.
- Ask for and give directions in a city.
- Write a message about a city visit.
- Design and talk about a new city.

I wonder... Which is the biggest city in the world?

1 market	2 hotel	3 shopping centre	4 ice rink	5 stadium
6 swimming pool	7 theatre	8 restaurant	9 funfair	10 art gallery

Lesson 1

Which places in the picture are in your city, too?

What can you see?

1 3.01 **Listen and find.**

2 3.02 **Listen and point. Then listen and repeat.**

3 **Watch and listen.**

4 **Look and say.**

shops cinema cars stadium pharmacy buses restaurant trees

There are some shops in the shopping centre.

There aren't any buses.

Song

We like going to the city,
Because it's fun, fun, fun!
We like going to the city,
Come on, everyone!

I like going to the ice rink,
I love going to the stadium, too.
I don't like going to the market,
Tell me! What about you?

Chorus

I like going to the swimming pool,
I love going to the theatre, too.
I don't like going to the funfair,
Tell me! What about you?

Chorus

I like going to the shopping centre,
I love going to the restaurant, too.
I don't like going to the art gallery,
Tell me! What about you?

Chorus

Lesson 2

1 3.03 Read and sing.

2 3.05 Listen, find and point.

3 Make sentences about the picture.

Grammar

I **like / love going** to the ice rink **because** it's amazing.	I **don't like going** to the market **because** it's boring.
He / She **likes / loves going** to the stadium **because** it's exciting.	He / She **doesn't like going** to the funfair **because** it's scary.

I can shine!

4 Where do you like going in your city? Why?

I like going to the art gallery because it's interesting.

I don't like going to the art gallery because it's boring! I love going to the market because it's exciting.

Me too! I love going to the market, too!

I can say where I like and don't like going in a city.

1 3.07 Listen, point and say.

1

watch a show

2

go to a restaurant

3

visit an exhibition

4

go shopping

5

watch a match

6

go on a ride

2 Which activities from Activity 1 can you see in the story?

3 3.08 Listen or watch. How do the children make the exhibition work?

Rise and Shine Museum

4 Read again and answer. *True* or *false*?

1 Eva makes this exhibition work.
2 Zoe is the first child to ride a bike.
3 The exhibition shows people and places in Future City.
4 Hugo likes going to the stadium.

I can shine!

5 Imagine you're at the exhibition. Talk about activities that you like and don't like doing.

I like watching a match but I don't like going shopping.

Me too! I like watching a match, too.

I can talk about activities that I like and don't like doing in a city.

Story value Understanding the importance of working together.

Lesson 4

1 3.09 Listen. What do they all like doing?

Look. Do you like doing these activities? Ask and answer.

2 3.10 Listen and read. Then chant.

Grammar builder

What do you like doing?	*I like… .*	
Do you like	*watching a show?*	
	going shopping?	*Yes, I do.*
	visiting an exhibition?	*No, I don't.*
	watching a match?	

go shopping
watch a show
visit an exhibition
take a photo
have a picnic
read a map

3 Look. Ask and answer.

Do you like watching a show?

Yes, I do!

Structures *What do you like doing? Do you like (watching a show)? Yes, I do. / No, I don't.*

Lesson 5

1 Look. Where do you like going?

2 3.11 Listen and follow the directions. Where is the art gallery on the map?

3 3.12 Listen again and repeat.

Pronunciation

4 3.13 Listen and say.

Excuse me, excuse me, excuse me,
Where's the city square?
Turn left, turn right, turn right, turn left,
The square is over there!

I can shine!

5 Ask your friend for directions.

Excuse me. Where's the playground?

Turn left and then turn right. Then go straight on.

I can ask for and give directions in a city.

Lesson 6

1 Look at the photos. Is your city the same or different?

2 3.15 Listen, read and match.

Rio de Janeiro Milan

THINGS TO DO | EVENTS | DEALS | GUIDES AND MAPS | RESTAURANTS

1

2

Green city fun!

We love having fun in our cities! There are always a lot of exciting things to do. Read about some children from around the world talking about what they like doing in their home cities. Which activity do you like best? What do you like doing in your city?

I like watching a football match. I love going to the Morro da Mineira stadium! It's a very clever stadium. When the football players run, the stadium lights work. I can play football there, too! It's a lot of fun!

David, Rio de Janeiro, Brazil

My friends and I enjoy planting trees in our big city. Some of the places in our city look ***boring***. We plant trees and then those places look ***lovely***! We love trees! They're beautiful!

Peter, London, UK

In my city, there are some amazing upcycling markets. I enjoy going shopping with my friends at these markets. We like using things again.

Idris, Port-au-Prince, Haiti

I don't like travelling by car in the city. Cars make our city ***dirty***. I like cycling with my friends. Bikes keep our city clean.

Aiko, Tokyo, Japan

I love doing a nature trail! And there's nature in my city, too. My aunt lives in the Bosco Verticale. These city towers have got trees and plants on them. They keep our city ***clean***, too.

Maria, Milan, Italy

3 Read again. Complete the sentences.

nature trees stadium market

1 David likes watching a match at the Morro da Mineira… .
2 Peter likes planting… in his city.
3 Idris likes going to the upcycling… .
4 Maria likes doing… trails.

4 3.16 Listen. Is Aiko's city clean?

5 3.17 Listen again and choose.

1 Aiko sees *interesting / boring* things when she cycles.
2 The Tokyo Skytree is a *tree / tower*.
3 Aiko's favourite season is *spring / summer*.
4 There are farms *on / under* the city towers.

Lesson 7

1 3.19 Listen and read. What does Aiko like watching?

Hi Dan,

I can't wait to see you next weekend! What do you like doing? Do you like watching a show? I love watching a show because it's exciting! But I don't enjoy watching a match because it's boring! What about you?

See you next weekend!

From,

Aiko

Our writing workshop

2 3.20 **Ideas generator** Listen, read and complete.

1 I like visiting...
because it's... !

2 I don't like going to...
because it's... !

3 I love going...
because it's... !

4 I don't like going on...
because it's... !

3 **Give it a go** Plan your message with a friend.

Where do you live? What do you like about it? What don't you like about it?

What do you like doing in your city? Why?

What don't you like doing in your city? Why?

I can shine!

4 Imagine that your friend is visiting your city next weekend. Write a message together.

I can write a message about a city visit.

Our new city

Step 1 Review

1 Look and say. Can you name more places?

There's a theatre!

2 Look again. Ask and answer.

Do you like going on a ride?

Yes, I do! I love going on a ride because it's exciting!

3 Ask for directions to a place in your city or town.

Excuse me. Where's the... ?

Turn left / right. Go... .

4 How can we keep our cities clean?

We can ride our bikes to school.

We can plant trees.

5 Watch and listen.

Step 2 Create

6 Which places do you want in your new city? Write a list.

7 Choose six places for your new city.

Let's put a market in our new city.

Let's put a stadium, too!

8 Create your new city map.

Time to shine!

9 Present your new city to the class.

This is our new city! There's a stadium. We like watching a match because it's fun!

10 Swap maps. Ask for and give directions.

Excuse me. Where's the… ?

11 Which new city would you like to live in? Why? Tell your friend.

I can design and talk about a new city.

4 Food for everyone!

Rise and Shine **Museum**

- Talk about different quantities of food.
- Understand a story about making a new dish.
- Ask and answer about the price of different food and drink.
- Write a no-waste shopping list.
- Create a no-waste café menu.

I wonder... Which vegetable can be orange, purple, red, white or yellow?

1 apples	2 grapes	3 pineapples	4 lemons	5 honey
6 potatoes	7 sugar	8 beans	9 rice	10 flour

Lesson 1

My favourite food is honey! What's your favourite food?

What can you see?

1 (4.01) **Listen and find.**

2 (4.02) **Listen and point. Then listen and repeat.**

3 **Watch and listen.**

4 **Look and say.**

I like potatoes but I don't like beans.

Song

Let's all eat together,
It's always a lot of fun!
Let's all eat together,
There's food for everyone!

There are a lot of potatoes,
There are many grapes,
There aren't any strawberries
But the apples are really great!

Chorus

There are some tasty beans,
There's a lot of rice,
There isn't any bread
But the honey is really nice!

Chorus

Lesson 2

1 4.03 Read and sing.

2 4.05 Listen and answer. *True* or *false*?

3 Make sentences about the picture.

Grammar	
There's some rice and a lot of honey.	There are a lot of potatoes, many grapes and some pineapples.
There isn't any bread.	There aren't any olives.

apples strawberries honey flour
carrots milk tomatoes cereal

I can shine!

4 Imagine a picnic for the class. Talk about the food.

There are a lot of honey sandwiches.

There are some tomatoes. There aren't any lemons.

I can talk about different quantities of food.

Lesson 3

1 4.07 Listen, point and say.

1

bag of rice

2

piece of fruit

3

box of fruit and vegetables

4

glass of water

5

cup of hot chocolate

6

bottle of juice

2 Look at the story. Which of the things in Activity 1 do the children find at the café?

3 4.08 Listen or watch. What do the children make for the café?

Rise and Shine Museum

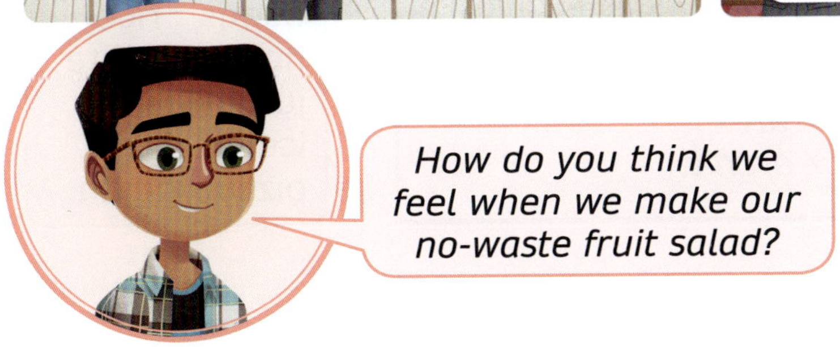

4 Read again and choose.

1. There's a lot of fruit in the *bag / box*.
2. The children make a rainbow salad from the *fruit / vegetables*.
3. The chef's name is *Marco / Ben*.
4. The children use apples, bananas, a pineapple, a lemon, strawberries and *grapes / rice*.

I can shine!

5 Imagine you're making a new dish. What do you want to make?

I want to make a salad with rice.

I want to make some pasta with beans.

I can understand a story about making a new dish for a no-waste café.

Lesson 4

1 4.10 Listen. What do Sofia and Hugo have for lunch?

2 4.11 Listen and read. Then chant.

Look. Ask and answer about the food and drink.

Grammar builder

		There are a lot of	
Are there any	*apples?*	*There's a box of*	*apples.*
Is there any	*rice?*	*There's a lot of*	*rice.*
		There are two bags of	
		Yes, there is / are. *No, there isn't / aren't.*	

carrots
beans rice
hot chocolate
juice milk
ice cream
pizza pasta

3 Look. Ask and answer.

bottle of	water
box of	strawberries
piece of	pizza
glass of	juice
bag of	sugar
cup of	hot chocolate

Are there any strawberries?

Yes, there are. There's a box of strawberries.

Structures *Are there any (apples)? Is there any (rice)?*

Lesson 5

1 Look. What food and drink can you see?

There is… .

There are… .

2 4.12 Listen, read and choose.

In the UK, people use *euros / pounds / dollars.*

3 4.13 Listen again and repeat.

Pronunciation

4 4.14 Listen and say.

How much is this big, brown cow?
How much is it? Please tell me now!

I can shine!

5 Ask and give prices for the things in Activity 1, page 46.

How much is this box of fruit?

It's £7.

How much are those apples?

They're £4.

I can ask and answer about the price of different food and drink.

Lesson 6

1 Does a no-waste café use all the food and drink?

2 4.15 Listen and read.

No-waste Café menu

About us

Welcome to our No-waste Café! Our food is very tasty. We don't waste any food. We use all our fruit and vegetables! Our chef makes all the things on our menu fresh every day for you to enjoy! So come and sit down, have a drink and try one of our special dishes. Enjoy our No-waste Café!

Our drinks

orange juice	**£1.50**
apple juice	**£1.75**
lemonade	**£1.99**
smoothie	**£2.99**
strawberry milkshake	**£3.25**
hot chocolate	**£2.25**

Our food

burger and chips	**£7.50**
fish and **chips**	**£6.99**
chicken pasta	**£8.50**
pizza with cheese, tomatoes and olives	**£8.00**
egg sandwich	**£4.99**
fruit salad with pineapple and grapes	**£4.99**
apple **cake**	**£3.75**
ice cream	**£3.50**
chocolate cookies	**£1.99**

3 Read again. Complete the sentences.

chicken pasta £1.50 ice cream £3.25 £6.99

1 The orange juice is… .
2 The… is £8.50.
3 The fish and chips are… .
4 The… is £3.50.
5 The strawberry milkshake is… .

4 4.16 Listen. Where does Louise work?

5 4.17 Read Louise's ideas. Listen again and number them in order.

- ☐ Write a no-waste shopping list.
- ☐ Go to a no-waste café.
- ☐ Buy boxes of ugly fruit and vegetables.

Lesson 7

1 4.20 Listen and read. How many people are there in Oliver's family?

My no-waste
Shopping List:

Four people in my family

8 apples	1 bag of grapes
8 carrots	8 eggs
12 potatoes	2 bottles of juice
1 pineapple	1 bag of rice

Oliver

Our writing workshop

2 4.21 **Ideas generator** Listen and match.

Hannah Michael Omar

1

2

3

3 **Give it a go** Plan your shopping list with a friend.

How many people are there in your family?

What food do they like?

How much food do they eat?

I can shine!

4 Write a no-waste shopping list for your family together.

I can write a no-waste shopping list.

My no-waste café menu

Step 1 Review

1 Look and name the different food and drink.

2 Look again. Ask and answer.

Are there any grapes?

Yes, there are. There are a lot of grapes.

3 Look. Ask and answer.

No-waste Café Menu

lemonade	$2.00
fruit smoothie	$3.50
apple juice	$2.75
hot chocolate	$2.99
milk	$1.25
burger and salad	$8.50
fish and chips	$10.99
chicken pasta	$9.50

How much is a lemonade?

It's $2.00.

4 How can we stop wasting food at home and at school?

We can make a no-waste shopping list when we go shopping.

Yes, that's a good idea. We can… .

5 Watch and listen.

Step 2 Create

6 Write a no-waste menu for one day.

My no-waste menu	
Breakfast	
Lunch	
Dinner	

7 Share your ideas.

8 Create a menu for a new no-waste café.

No-waste café menu

Our drinks

lemonade £2.50
fruit smoothie £3.00

Our food

rice and vegetables £7.99
egg sandwich £4.99

Time to shine!

9 Show your menu to the class. Ask and answer.

10 Choose a menu. You have £10. What do you want to eat and drink?

I can create a no-waste café menu.

Review 2 Our community

1 4.24 Listen. What do the children want to put inside the time capsule?

2 Look. Ask and answer.

watch a show go on a ride visit an exhibition go shopping	pineapples grapes apples lemons carrots potatoes honey rice sugar

Do you like... + -ing?

Is there any... ?

Are there any... ?

3 Write a no-waste recipe with a friend.

4 Read. Name three places in Sofia's city.

I'm Sofia. I love our city! I like watching a show at the theatre but I don't like going on a scary ride at the funfair. Today, there's a no-waste market in our city. There's a lot of fruit. There are some boxes of vegetables, too. I like going shopping at the market. What do you like doing in your city?

5 Write about activities you like doing in your city or town.

MINI PROJECT

6 ✏ **Plan a no-waste city picnic.**

- Ask and answer about food you need for the picnic.

Is there any... ?

- Choose a place to have your picnic.

Do you like going to the... ?

7 **Present your ideas to the class.**

This is our no-waste picnic. There are some sandwiches, some strawberries and a lot of grapes.

Time to shine!

8 **What can you see in the exhibitions? Complete your Museum Trail Card.**

Museum Trail Card

1	I can read, write and say places in a town and food.
2	I can say what I like doing in my city and talk about food.
3	I can ask for and give street directions.
4	I can ask and answer about prices.

Rise and Shine Museum

City of the future

Food for everyone!

5 Help our oceans!

Museum

- Talk about what different animals are doing.
- Talk about looking after the oceans.
- Ask for and give information about an event.
- Write a poster about a beach clean up.
- Create a play about helping the oceans.

I wonder... What is Kids' Ocean Day?

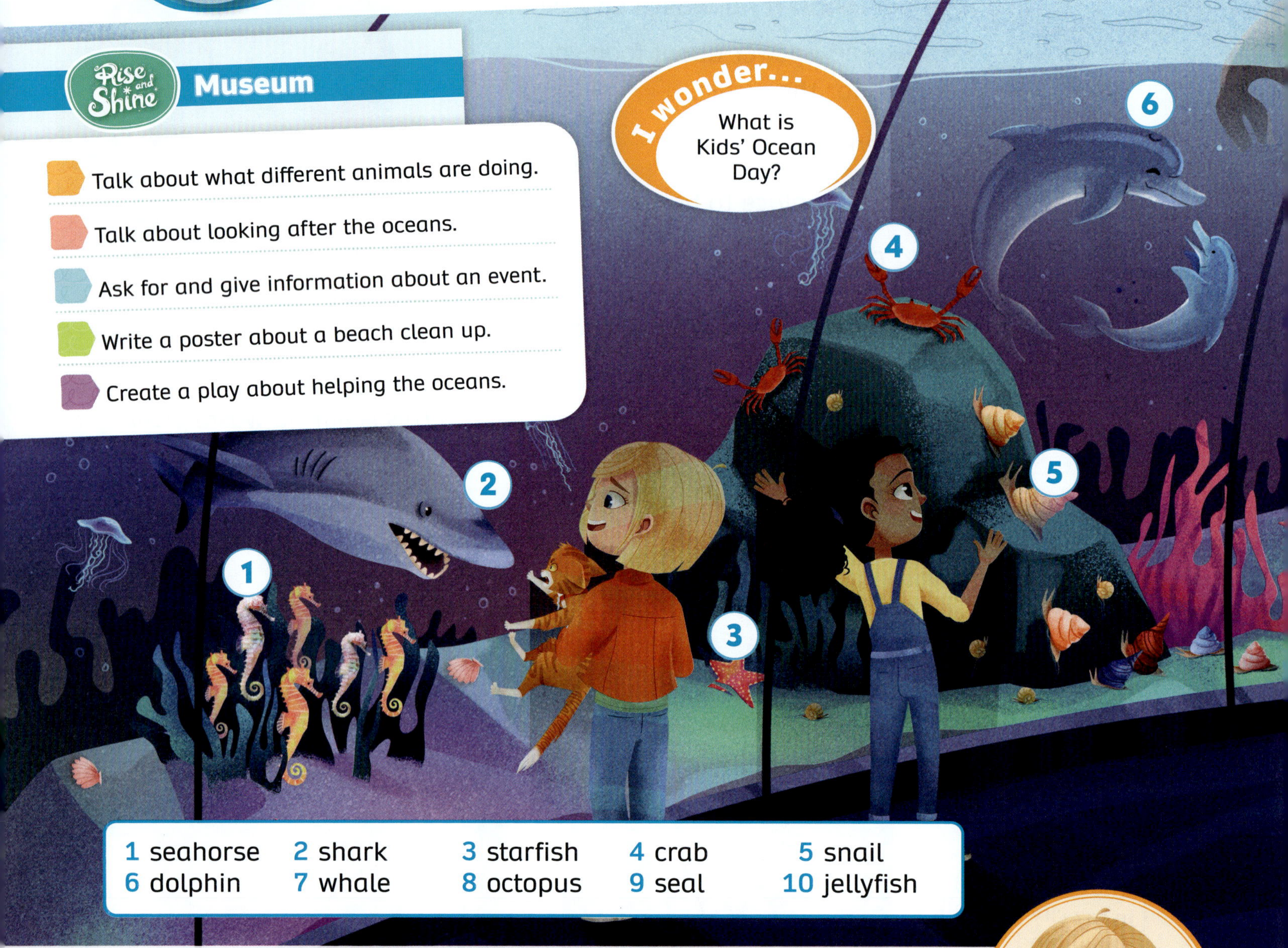

1 seahorse	2 shark	3 starfish	4 crab	5 snail
6 dolphin	7 whale	8 octopus	9 seal	10 jellyfish

Lesson 1

What's your favourite sea animal? Why?

What can you see?

1 5.01 **Listen and find.**

2 5.02 **Listen and point. Then listen and repeat.**

3 **Watch and listen.**

4 **Ask and answer.**

some any a lot of many

Are there any snails?

Yes, there are. There are some snails.

Song

Ocean animals are sometimes big,
Seals, sharks and whales!
Ocean animals are sometimes small,
Starfish, jellyfish and snails!

I can see some starfish!
They've got arms but they haven't got hands.
They aren't swimming in the sea.
They're hiding in the sand!

Chorus

I can see some crabs!
They've got legs but they haven't got paws.
They aren't hiding in the sand.
They're waving with their claws!

Chorus

I can see some seals!
They've got hands and they've got feet.
They aren't playing with a ball.
They're sleeping in the sea!

Chorus

Lesson 2

1 5.03 Read and sing.

2 5.05 Listen and answer. *True* or *false*?

3 Make sentences about the picture.

Grammar

The shark **is** swimm**ing**. It **isn't** walk**ing**.
The starfish **are** hid**ing**. They **aren't** jump**ing**.

I can shine!

4 Choose one of the sea animals. Act and guess.

They're dolphins! They're playing.

I can talk about what different animals are doing.

Lesson 3

1 5.07 Listen, point and say.

1

clean the oceans

2

have a beach clean up

3

pick up rubbish

4

recycle rubbish

5

make a film

6

tell people

2 Look at the story. Which activities from Activity 1 can you see?

3 5.08 Listen or watch. How do the children want to help the oceans?

4 Read again and complete the sentences.

beaches poster rubbish Socks

1 The seals are eating the… .
2 The people are cleaning the… .
3 … is picking up rubbish in the museum.
4 The children are making a… about a beach clean up.

I can shine!

5 Imagine you are at the exhibition. How can you help the oceans?

We can have a beach clean up.

We can make a film about ocean rubbish.

I can talk about looking after the oceans.

Lesson 4

1 5.09 Listen. What are Zoe and Marco doing?

2 5.10 Listen and read. Then chant.

Look at the picture. Point, ask and answer.

Grammar builder

What are they doing?	*They're picking up rubbish.*	
Are they	*cleaning the beach?*	*Yes, they are.*
	playing on the beach?	*No, they aren't.*

Zoe and Marco / swim
the seals / sleep
those children / recycling rubbish
the dolphins / jump

3 Look. Ask and answer.

1

2

3

4

What are they doing?

They're making a film.

Structures *What are they doing? They're (making a film). Are they (picking up rubbish)?*

Lesson 5

1 5.11 Listen. When is the beach clean up?

1 *Excuse me! When is the beach clean up?*

2 *It's on Sunday.*

3 *What time does it start?*

4 *It starts at ten o'clock.*

5 *OK, great. Where is it?*

6 *It's on Sunny Beach.*

2 5.12 Listen again and repeat.

Pronunciation

5 5.15 Listen and say.

The clean up was yesterday. Was it good fun?
Yes, it was! It was fun in the sun.

3 5.13 Listen and read. What day is it today?

Boy	Look. There's a beach clean up! When is it?
Girl	It was on Sunday. It was yesterday!
Boy	Oh! Were you at the clean up?
Girl	Yes, I was. It was interesting.
Boy	Was it fun?
Girl	No, it wasn't. It was a lot of work but it was good to help the ocean.
Boy	Were Adam and Holly at the clean up?
Girl	Yes, they were.

4 5.14 Listen again and answer.

1 When was the beach clean up?
2 Was it interesting? Was it fun?
3 Were Adam and Holly at the clean up?

I can shine!

6 Think of some events, days and times. Ask and answer.

What time does the picnic start?

It starts at three o'clock.

I can ask for and give information about an event.

Lesson 6

1 Look at the pictures. What can you see?

BEN'S BLOG:

Hello! I'm Ben and I'm ten years old. Welcome to my blog! I like writing about the world around us. I hope you enjoy reading my blog.

3rd March

Today, I want to talk about our oceans! There's a lot of rubbish in the ocean. This rubbish is **dangerous** for the animals! How can young people help? Let's find out!

Clean the oceans!

Boyan Slat from the Netherlands has got an Ocean Clean Up project. His team pick up rubbish in the oceans. Then they recycle the rubbish. It's a **brilliant** project!

Make a film!

Some school children from Hawaii, USA, are making a film. The film is about rubbish in the ocean. There's a lot of plastic rubbish on the beaches in Hawaii. It's a **terrible** problem. It isn't **safe** for the animals in the ocean. This film is a great way to tell people about ocean rubbish.

Go to a beach clean up!

It's Kids' Ocean Day in Los Angeles, USA. Look! There are four thousand children at a beach clean up! They're picking up rubbish. They're making a big picture on the beach, too. What animal can you see?

All these young people are helping the oceans but everyone can help. And I want to help, too! Let's have a clean up at our beach!

Is there a beach, a park or a forest near your home? Can you help to clean it up?

2 5.16 Listen and read. Choose the best title for the blog post.

a Animals in the ocean
b Young people and the oceans
c My holiday by the ocean

3 Read again. Answer the questions.

1 How old is Ben?
2 Where does Boyan Slat come from?
3 What are the children from Hawaii doing?
4 What are the children from Los Angeles doing?

4 5.17 Listen. Which event from Ben's blog does the man talk about?

5 5.18 Listen again and choose.

1 The beach clean up is at *Seal Beach / Whale Beach*.
2 The plastic rubbish *is / isn't* dangerous for sea animals.
3 The beach clean up is on Saturday *3rd / 13th* July.
4 The beach clean up starts at *ten / two* o'clock in the morning.

Lesson 7

1 5.20 Listen and read. What event is Ben's poster for?

Where? Sunny Beach
When? Sunday 4th August
What time? 9.00-12.00

Come and help!

This is our beautiful beach. Let's clean it up!

We can help the seals, dolphins and whales.

We can pick up rubbish from the beach and we can recycle it.

See you at nine o'clock in front of New Hotel!

Our writing workshop

2 5.21 Ideas generator
Listen and match.

Luis Jen Ben Ola

1

2

3

4

3 Give it a go Plan your poster with a friend.

- Where is your clean up?
- Which day is your clean up?
- What time does it start? What time does it finish?
- Where do people meet?

I can shine!

4 Write your poster about a beach clean up together.

I can write a poster about a beach clean up.

Our ocean play

Step 1 Review

1 What are they doing? Can you name other sea animals?

The seals are playing.

Those children are picking up rubbish.

2 Look again. Ask, answer and guess.

Are they having a no-waste picnic?

No, they aren't.

3 Look. Ask and answer about the beach clean up.

4 How can you help the oceans?

We can pick up our rubbish.

5 Watch and listen.

Step 2 Create

6 Which are your favourite sea animals? What can they do?

Dolphins are my favourite sea animals. They're beautiful! They can swim and they can jump!

7 How can you help the animals in the ocean?

We can pick up rubbish.

We can make a film about rubbish in the ocean.

8 Create and act out a play in your group.

Time to shine!

9 Share your play with the class! Guess what the other children are doing.

10 Which play has the most ideas?

I can create a play about helping the oceans.

6 Let's play together!

Rise and Shine Museum

- Talk about sports I'm going / not going to do.
- Talk about a team race.
- Make a plan to do sports with a friend.
- Write a note to a friend about an unusual sport.
- Plan a sports weekend.

1 play baseball
2 go snowboarding
3 go swimming
4 do athletics
5 play hockey
6 play volleyball
7 play basketball
8 play table tennis
9 play badminton
10 do gymnastics

Lesson 1

What can you see?

1 6.01 **Listen and find.**

2 6.02 **Listen and point. Then listen and repeat.**

3 **Watch and listen.**

4 **Look, point and say.**

That boy is playing hockey.

Those children are doing athletics.

Song

Let's do sport together.
Let's run, let's jump, let's play!
Let's have fun together.
Let's do sport every day!

I'm not going to go swimming,
I don't like going to the pool.
I'm going to do athletics.
Do you want to do that, too?

Chorus

I'm not going to play badminton,
I don't like playing that game.
I'm going to play volleyball.
Do you want to do the same?

Chorus

I'm not going to go snowboarding,
I don't like playing in the snow.
I'm going to play table tennis.
Do you want to have a go?

Chorus

Lesson 2

1 6.03 Read and sing.

2 6.05 Listen, find and point.

3 Imagine you're at the exhibition. Make sentences about the picture.

Grammar

I'm going to play table tennis.
I'm not going to do gymnastics.

I can shine!

4 Talk about sports you're going to do next week.

I'm going to play hockey. I'm not going to go swimming.

I can talk about sports I'm going to do and sports I'm not going to do.

Lesson 3

1 6.08 Listen, point, and say.

1

jump hurdles

2

run a race

3

win a race

4

hit a ball

5

throw a ball

6

bounce a ball

2 Which activities do you think the children are going to do in the story? Write.

They are going to ________________

________________________________.

3 6.09 Listen or watch.
Which team wins the race?

4 Read again and answer. *True* or *false*?

1 The Museum Champions' Race is a race for one child.
2 Marco doesn't want to run the race.
3 Hugo is good at jumping hurdles.
4 Zoe wants to hit the ball in the race.
5 Sofia goes fourth in the race.

I can shine!

5 Imagine the race. Who is going to go first, second, third and fourth? Why?

I'm going to go second. I like playing basketball! I'm good at bouncing the ball!

I can talk about a team race.

Lesson 4

1 6.10 Listen. What sport is Sofia going to do next weekend?

2 6.11 Listen and read. Then chant.

Grammar builder

What are you going to do?	*I'm going to play volleyball.*	
Are you going to	*play table tennis?*	*No, I'm not.*
	do gymnastics?	*Yes, I am.*

Look. Are you going to do these activities next week? Ask and answer.

3 Look. Ask and answer.

Are you going to play hockey next week?

No, I'm not. I'm going to do gymnastics.

	✓	✗
1	do gymnastics	play hockey
2	jump hurdles	run a race
3	bounce a ball	throw a ball
4	do athletics	go swimming
5	go snowboarding	play badminton

Structures *What are you going to do? Are you going to (do gymnastics)? Yes, I am. / No, I'm not.*

Lesson 5

1 Look. What sports can you see?

2 6.12 Listen and read.

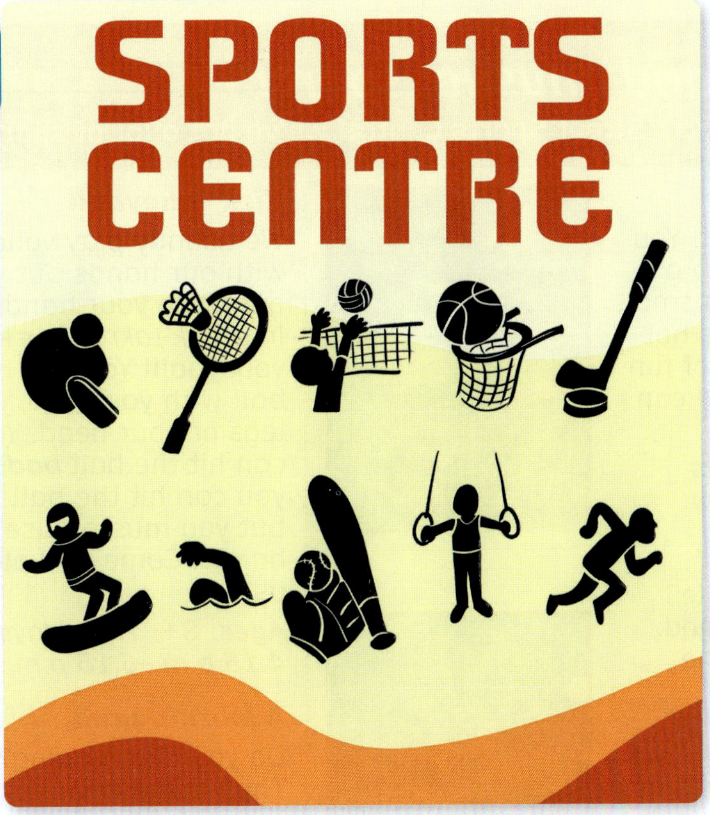

1 *Hi, Sam! Are you free on Thursday afternoon?*

2 *No, I'm not. Sorry!*

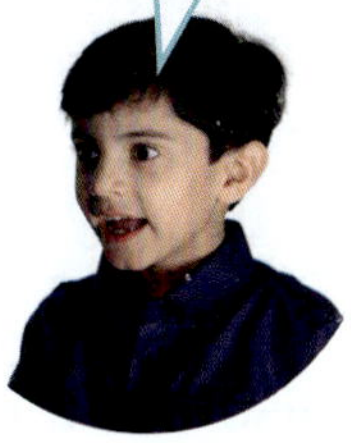

1 *Hi, Jo! Are you free on Thursday afternoon?*

2 *Yes, I am!*

3 *Do you want to do athletics with me?*

4 *Yes, please! See you then!*

5 *Great! Bye!*

3 6.13 Listen again and repeat.

Pronunciation

4 6.14 Listen and say.

I think these three brothers do athletics on Thursdays with their father and mother!

I can shine!

5 Plan to do some sports with your friend.

Hi! Are you free on... ?

Do you want to... ?

I can make a plan to do sports with a friend.

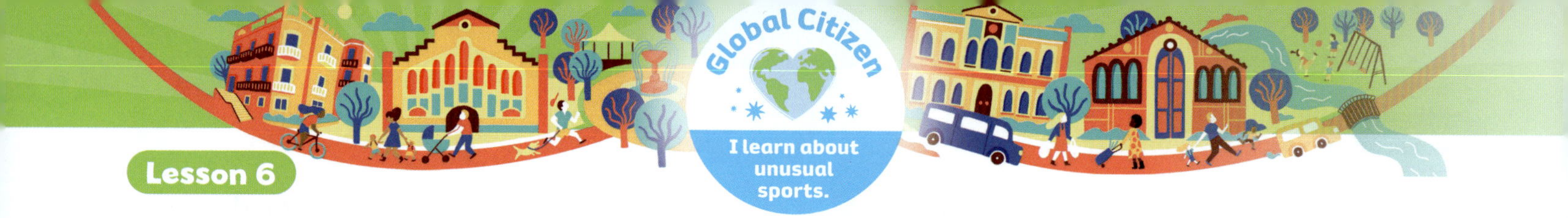

Lesson 6

1 Do you do any unusual sports?

2 6.15 Listen and read.

Try a new and unusual sport!

Come and visit North Street Sports Centre! We've got a lot of sports for you to try!

Disc golf

Let's play disc golf! You don't hit a ball into a hole – you throw a small disc into a net! It's not easy but it's a lot of fun and a lot of people can play.

Ages: 8+; Tuesdays 4.00 p.m.–5.00 p.m.

Team table tennis

It's fun to play table tennis with one friend. It's fun to play table tennis with a lot of friends, too! At North Street Sports Centre, you can play table tennis in a team. You hit the ball and then run around the table. It's interesting and a lot of fun. Come and have a go!

Ages: 8–10; Wednesdays 4.00 p.m.–5.00 p.m.

Kick volleyball

We usually play volleyball with our hands but you can't use your hands in *sepak takraw*, or kick volleyball! You can hit the ball with your feet, your legs or your head. You can hit the ball ***badly*** or you can hit the ball ***well*** but you mustn't use your hands! Come and play with us!

Ages: 8+; Thursdays 4.15 p.m.–5.15 p.m.

A morning run

Do you like running? Then come and run with us before school every morning. We all run together as a team! Sometimes we run ***quickly*** and sometimes we run ***slowly***. We run in the sun and we run in the rain. It's a great way to start the day! Come too!

Ages: 8–16; every morning 7.30 a.m.–8.00 a.m.

North Street Sports Centre
Stay happy and healthy

3 Read and choose.

1 You can play disc golf on *Tuesdays / Thursdays*.

2 Team table tennis is on *Mondays / Wednesdays*.

3 You can use your *hands / feet* in kick volleyball.

4 You can run every *morning / afternoon*.

4 6.16 Listen. Which sport are they going to do together next week?

5 6.17 Listen again and complete.

1 Ethan's favourite sport is... .

2 Ethan is going to play... next week.

3 Ava thinks the team table tennis looks... .

4 They are going to meet at... on Wednesday.

Lesson 7

1 6.19 **Listen and choose.**

Ava is writing to Diego about…

a the unusual sports at the new sports centre.

b playing team table tennis together at the new sports centre.

c how to get to the new sports centre.

Hi Diego,
I'm going to play table tennis with Ethan at the new sports centre next Wednesday. It's team table tennis! It is difficult but it looks fun!
Are you free on Wednesday afternoon? Do you want to play team table tennis with us?
The sports centre is on North Street.
Team table tennis is from four o'clock to five o'clock.

I hope you can come!

Bye,

Ava

Our writing workshop

2 6.20 Ideas generator **Listen, read and complete.**

1

I'm writing about running in the… .

2

I'm writing about snowboarding in the… .

3

I'm writing about playing volleyball in the… .

4

I'm writing about playing basketball in the… .

3 Give it a go **Plan to write a note with a friend.**

Which unusual sport are you going to do?

Why is it unusual?

Where are you going to do it?

What time are you going to do it?

I can shine!

4 **Write your note about an unusual sport together.**

I can write a note to a friend about an unusual sport.

Our sports weekend

Step 1 Review

1 Look and write the sports.

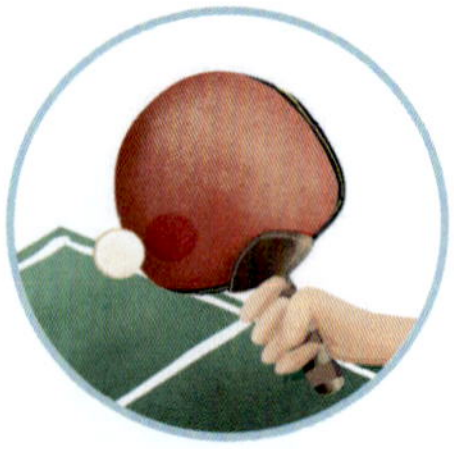    

2 Choose a sport. Ask, answer, and guess.

Are you going to hit the ball?

No, I'm not.

Are you going to bounce the ball?

Yes, I am.

Are you going to play basketball?

Yes, I am. Good job!

3 Look again. Make a plan to play one of the sports together next weekend.

Hi! Are you free on… ?

Do you want to… ?

4 Why is it good to work as a team?

You can help your friends.

Yes and you can… .

5 Watch and listen.

Step 2 Create

6 Create a sports weekend.

	Saturday	Sunday
Morning		
Afternoon		
Evening		

7 Share your ideas.

*I'm going to play basketball on Saturday morning. What are **you** going to do?*

8 Decide which sports you are going to do together.

Time to shine!

9 Present your sports weekend to the class.

10 Choose two new sports to try.

On Saturday morning, we are going to do gymnastics.

On Saturday afternoon, we are going to play hockey.

I can plan a sports weekend.

Review 3 Our world

1 6.22 Listen. What are the children going to put inside the time capsule?

2 Look. Ask and answer. *What are those children doing?*

3 Imagine you're at the beach. What are you going to do?

4 How can we help the oceans?

5 Read. Where is Zoe going to go today?

Dear Holly,
I'm going to go to the beach today.
I'm not going to go swimming. I'm going to have a beach clean up with my friends. I'm going to pick up rubbish and I'm going to recycle it. Then I'm going to play volleyball. I love playing volleyball! It's great to play in a team. I'm going to have a wonderful time.
What are you going to do today?

From,
Zoe

6 Read again and choose.

1. Zoe is going to go out with her *friends / family* today.
2. She's going to *go swimming / pick up rubbish.*
3. She *likes / doesn't like* playing volleyball.
4. She *thinks / doesn't think* she's going to have a good time today.

7 Imagine you're going to go to the beach today. Write a postcard to a friend about what you're going to do.

MINI PROJECT

8 Plan a beach clean up and some team sports.

- How are you going to clean up the beach?
- Which team sports are you going to do?

9 Present your ideas to the class.

Today, I'm going to clean up the beach with my friends. I'm going to pick up rubbish and I'm going to make a film about it, too! Then I'm going to do some team sports. I'm going to play badminton and hockey!

Time to shine!

10 What can you see in the exhibitions? Complete your Museum Trail Card.

Museum Trail Card

1	I can read, write and say the names of ocean animals and sports.
2	I can ask and answer about sports activities and make plans.
3	I can ask and say when and where an event is.
4	I can make plans with friends.

Rise and Shine Museum

Help our oceans!

Let's play together!

Goodbye from The Rise and Shine Museum

What can you see?

1 7.01 Listen or watch. Which five things do the children put inside the time capsule?

2 7.02 Listen again. Which words do you hear?

flower pot cup strawberries storybook octopus turtle
hockey basketball pineapple art gallery moustache smile

Song

It's the Rise and Shine Museum.
Come on! Let's explore!
It's the Rise and Shine Museum.
Exhibitions on every floor!

We love visiting the museum.
We always see interesting things.
We do a lot of different activities.
We act, we play, we sing!

Chorus

But it's time to say goodbye now.
Goodbye Eva and Socks, too.
Goodbye, goodbye, children.
And goodbye, goodbye to you!

Chorus

Test your progress with English Benchmark Young Learners

3 7.03 Read and sing.

4 Ask and answer.

Who's your favourite character in Rise and Shine?

I like Marco because he's funny and clever.

Which is your favourite unit?

I like Unit 5 because I love our oceans!

I can shine!

5 Choose four more things to put inside your time capsule. Tell the class.

I'm going to put a book about sharks inside my time capsule. I think sharks are brilliant!

I'm going to put a football inside my time capsule. I love playing football!

Museum Takeover Day

1 clean the museum
2 welcome visitors
3 cook in the museum café
4 work as a tour guide
5 help in the museum shop
6 plan an exhibition

1 8.01 **Listen. What's for lunch today?**

a pasta b pizza c potatoes

2 8.02 **Listen and point. Then listen and repeat.**

3 8.03 **Listen, read and say. Then join in.**

It's Museum Takeover Day.
Children... everything!
We help, we..., we clean, we...
And then, of course, we... !

4 **Make a Museum Takeover Day brochure. Draw and write.**

5 **Plan your own Museum Takeover Day.**

Our Museum Takeover Day

Start – 9.00 a.m.
Clean the museum – José
Work as a tour guide – Mariam
Welcome visitors – Irem
Help in the museum shop – Davide
Finish – 4.00 p.m.

I'm going to work as a tour guide! What do you want to do on Museum Takeover Day?

World Food Day

1 eat a healthy diet
2 eat a lot of fruit and vegetables
3 choose brown food
4 drink a lot of water
5 don't eat a lot of sugar
6 don't eat junk food

1 8.05 Listen. Which food are the children sharing?

a sandwiches b apples c beans

2 8.06 Listen and point. Then listen and repeat.

3 8.07 Listen, read and say. Then join in.

We all love World Food...,
We learn about healthy food.
We love... vegetables
And we love rapping, ... !

4 Make a healthy eating poster.

International Day of Forests

1 8.09 Listen. What do the children want to build?

a a den   b a path   c a gate

2 8.10 Listen and point. Then listen and repeat.

3 8.11 Listen, read and say. Then join in.

It's International… of Forests,
Forests are… everyone!
Let's… a tree together,
Then let's all have… !

4 Make a forest walk poster.

I'm planting a tree! What do you want to do on International Day of Forests?

Museum Open Day

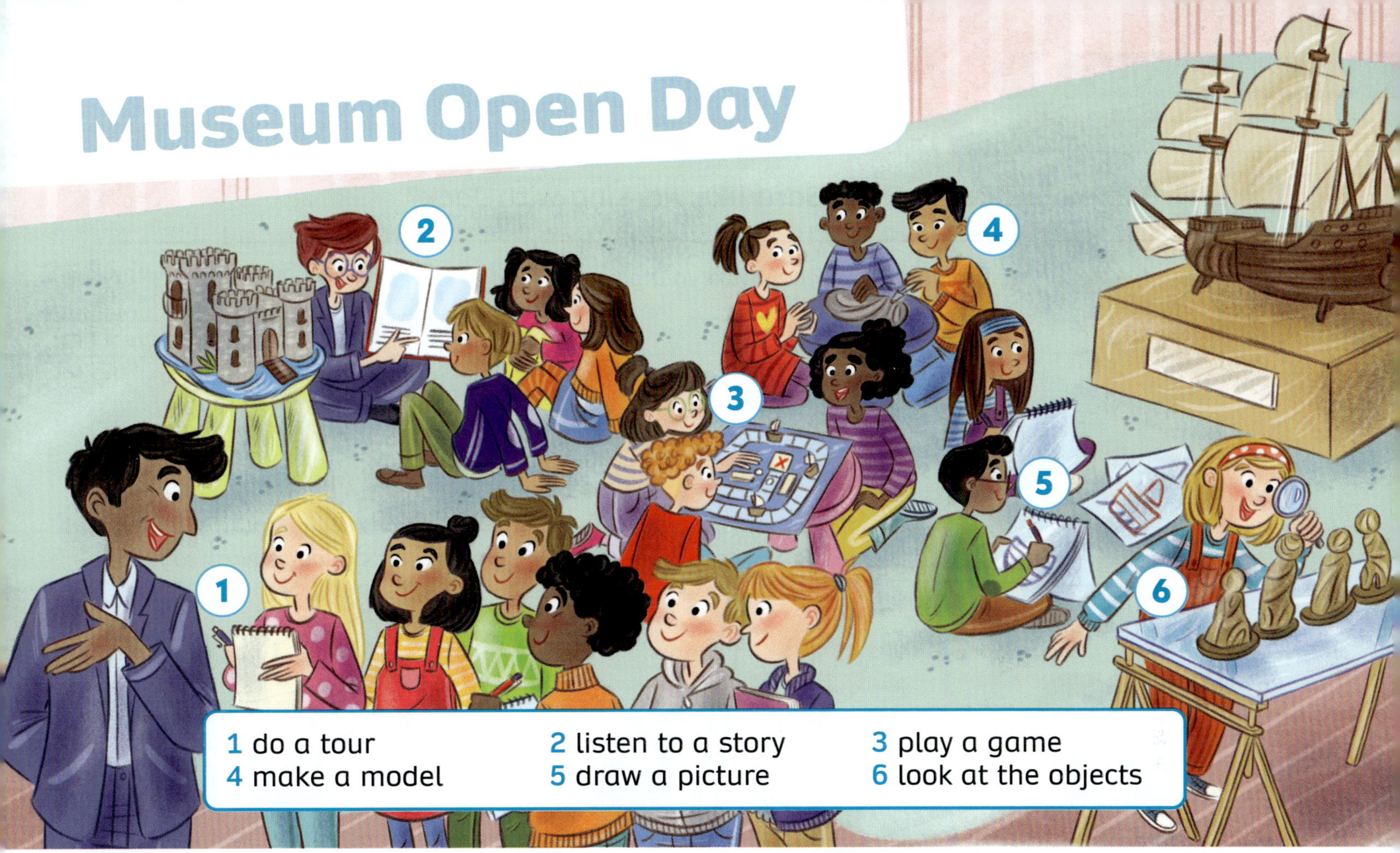

1 do a tour
2 listen to a story
3 play a game
4 make a model
5 draw a picture
6 look at the objects

1 8.13 **Listen. What is Dina going to do?**

a play a game

b make a model

c look at the objects

2 8.14 **Listen and point. Then listen and repeat.**

3 8.15 **Listen, read and say. Then join in.**

... is Museum Open Day,
We stay... all day... !
We play, we listen, we..., we make
And... we sing a... !

4 **Act out a Museum Open Day. Ask and answer.**

Would you like to listen to a story about an old castle?

Yes, I would! I'd like to draw a picture, too.

Would you like to go to the Museum Open Day? Why? Why not?

1 9.01 Listen and read. Does Sara like working with Jack?

2 Why does Jack help Sara?

a Sara thinks the work is difficult.
b Sara doesn't understand the work.
c Sara doesn't want help.

3 Imagine you want to help someone. What can you say?

– Can I help you?
– I want to help.
– …
– …

Useful language

What can I do? How can I help you?
Let's work together / think of some ideas.
Shall we work together?

Time to shine!

4 Imagine and act out.

Your friend can't come to play football on Saturday.

I want to play football but I've got a lot of homework.

Can I help you?

Yes, please! I can't do this question.

Reflect How can your friends help you?

1 9.02 Listen and read. Why don't Tiger and Turtle want to work together?

2 What do Tiger and Turtle learn?

a We are different inside.
b We are the same inside.

3 How can we respect others?

- Listen.
- Be kind.
- ...
- ...

Useful language

I like / enjoy working with you.
Thank you. It's good to work with you.
Let's... . You're welcome.

Time to shine!

4 Imagine and act out.

Your friend doesn't like her new classmate. What do you do?

I don't like the new girl.
Let's go and say hello to her together.
Hello! What's your name?
It's good to be friends.

Reflect Are you friends with everyone in your class?

1 Listen and read. Why is there a problem?

9.03

2 How do they feel at the end of the story? Why?

3 How can we talk to each other?

- Ask questions.
- Listen to each other.
- Talk about how you feel.
- …
- …

Useful language

What do you want to do? What can I do?
Let's talk to each other.
Let's work together / as a team.
I feel happy / sad.

Time to shine!

4 Imagine and act out.

What can you do every day?

I say hello to my teacher in the morning.

I talk to my friends at lunch.

Reflect What should you do when you work in a group?

1 Listen and read. What does the teacher ask the class to do?

9.04

2 Read and choose for Jack and Zain.

Jack I *am / am not* looking after the flower. I *am / am not* responsible.

Zain I *am / am not* looking after the flower. I *am / am not* responsible.

3 How can we be responsible?

- Listen to others.
- Think about what others need.
- Think about how we can help others.
- ...
- ...

Useful language

What do you need?	How do I look after... ?
What do I need to do?	I'm going to look after... .

Time to shine!

4 Imagine and act out.

How can you be responsible?

I can make my own breakfast.

I can do all my homework.

Reflect When you are responsible, how do you feel?

1 Listen and read. How does Jack feel?

9.05

2 How does Zain help?

a Zain tells Jack to go home.
b Zain wears skiing clothes with Jack.
c Zain laughs at Jack.

3 How can you help someone feel good?

- Ask if they are OK.
- Smile.
- Be kind.
- …
- …

Useful language

Are you OK?	Don't feel bad / sad!
Don't worry!	I understand!

Time to shine!

4 Imagine and act out.

Your friend feels sad. What do you do?

I feel sad today. I can't find my favourite toy.

I understand. Let's try to find it.

Reflect How can people help you when you feel sad?

1 Listen and read. What doesn't Keira like?

9.06

2 What happens at the end of the story? Write the sentence.

eating / enjoys / Keira / carrots. / the

3 How can we learn to be open-minded?

- Eat new food.
- Meet new people.
- Do new activities.
- …
- …

Useful language

You're going to love it / them!
It's / They're good / fun. Let's… .
Shall we try it / them? It's good because… .

Time to shine!

4 Imagine and act out.

Your friend doesn't like sports. You want to do sports with them. What do you do?

I don't like sports. I think they're boring.

Let's play badminton. It's fun. You're going to love it!

Reflect What don't you like? Can you change your mind? Why? Why not?

1 Read and complete.

has   hasn't   Has   hasn't   got   look

REMEMBER!
He's got / She's got / It's got… .
Remember to say the 's'!

What does your town [1]… like?

[3]… it got a sports centre?

Has it [5]… a hospital?

It's got a beautiful park but it [2]… got a lake.

Yes, it [4]… .

No, it [6]… .

2 10.01 Listen and choose.

1 a  b 

2 a  b 

3 a  b 

3 Write about your town.

My town is… .

It's got… .   It hasn't got… .

Grammar
What has your town got?
It's got a river.
Has it got a theatre?
Yes, it has. / No, it hasn't.

4 Ask and answer.

What has your town got?

It's got a cinema and it's got some cafés.

Grammar 2

REMEMBER!

Smile to help you say *these*.

1 Read and complete.

those   these   mine   yours

Whose are [1]... shoes?

Those shoes are mine.
Are these trainers [2]... ?

No, [3]... trainers aren't mine. They're hers.

That's right! Those trainers are [4]... .

2 10.02 Listen and match.

1 glasses — a Kate

2 watch — b Maria

3 trousers — c Joe

4 trainers — d Adam

Grammar

Is this your coat?
Yes, it is. / No, it isn't.
Are these your shoes?
Yes, they are. / No, they aren't.

3 Whose are these things? Look and write.

That... is... .   Those... are... .

4 Ask and answer about your things.

Is this your scarf?

Yes, it is. That's my scarf.
Are these your trainers?

No, they aren't. They're his.
These are mine.

1 Read and complete.

No Do do like What

[1]... do you like doing?

[3]... you like going to the forest?

I [2]... going to the lake. I love swimming!

Yes, I [4]... . / [5]..., I don't.

REMEMBER!

Do you like going to the park?

2 10.03 Listen and choose.

1 Peter *likes* / *doesn't like* going to the playground.

2 Jemma *likes* / *doesn't like* going to the countryside.

3 Peter *likes* / *doesn't like* going to the forest.

4 Jemma *likes* / *doesn't like* going to the beach.

3 What do you like doing? Write.

I like... but I don't like... .

I like... and I love... .

Grammar

Do you like going to the beach?
Yes, I do. / No, I don't.
Why do you like going to the beach?
I like going to the beach because it's fun.

4 Ask and answer.

What do you like doing?

I like going to the mountains but I don't like going to the lake.

Why do you like going to the mountains?

I like going to the mountains because it's exciting!

1 Read and complete.

isn't there Yes are Is Are

REMEMBER!

There **are** a lot of / many / some cafés.

[1]... there any restaurants in your town?

[4]... there a theatre in your town?

[2]..., there are. There [3]... a lot of restaurants.

No, there [5]... but [6]... are some cinemas.

2 Read and answer the questions.

My town is very big. There's a shopping centre and there are a lot of different shops. There are a lot of cafés but there aren't any restaurants. There's a theatre next to the shopping centre and there's a restaurant in the theatre. There isn't a cinema in my town but there's a big stadium. There are two sports centres.

1. Are there a lot of cafés?
2. Is there a theatre?
3. Are there any cinemas?
4. Are there any sports centres?
5. Is there a restaurant in the shopping centre?

Grammar

What is there in your town?
There's a cinema. **There aren't many** shops.
There aren't any theatres.

3 Write about your town.

There are many... in my town.

There isn't... . There aren't many... .

There are a lot of... but there aren't many / any... .

4 Ask and answer.

Are there any art galleries in your town?

No, there aren't but there are a lot of museums. What is there in your town?

There are a lot of sports centres but there isn't an ice rink.

1 Read and complete.

are Yes are Are aren't those

What [1]… those children doing?

They're at the beach. They [2]… windsurfing but they aren't sailing.

[3]… those girls swimming?

[4]…, they are. Are [5]… boys fishing?

No, they [6]… .

REMEMBER!

They **are not** sailing. = They **aren't** sailing.

2 10.04 Listen and answer. *True* or *false*?

1 They are rock-climbing.
2 They aren't doing a nature trail.
3 They aren't swimming.
4 They are skateboarding.

3 It is Saturday afternoon. Look and write.

They are… .

They aren't… .

4 Ask and answer.

Are they kayaking?

Yes, they are.

5 The activities in Activity 3 were yesterday. Write sentences.

The boys were kayaking on the lake yesterday.

Grammar

They're swimm**ing** at the beach.
Are they windsurf**ing**?
Yes, they are. / **No, they aren't.**
Was Peter at the sea yesterday?
Yes, he was. / **No, he wasn't.**
Were they in the forest yesterday?
Yes, they were. / **No, they weren't.**

REMEMBER!

I'm not going to use the computer.

1 Read and complete.

to What I'm going not

¹… are you going to do this weekend?

Are you going ⁴… play chess?

I'm ²… to stay at home but I'm ³… going to play computer games.

Yes, I am. / No,⁵… not.

2 10.05 Read. Then listen and tick (✓) or cross (✗).

	Ilona	Mike
learn something new		
do sport		
paint		
help people		
take photos		
play the drums		
be outside		

3 What you are going to do next weekend? Think and write.

I'm going to… . I'm not going to… .

Grammar

Are you going to play football at the weekend?
Yes, I am. / No, I'm not.
When are you going to play football?
I'm going to play football on Saturday.

4 Ask and answer.

Are you going to play computer games?

Yes, I am.

When are you going to play computer games?

I'm going to play computer games this evening.

The Rise and Shine Museum Trail

Look at… cups!
These are… !
3
Complete Hugo's sentences.
4
What can you see?
5
There are lots of / many / some… .

Pearson Education Limited
KAO Two
KAO Park
Hockham Way
Harlow, Essex
CM17 9SR
England
and Associated Companies throughout the world.

pearsonenglish.com

First published 2021
Seventh impression 2024

ISBN: 978-1-292-36931-0

Set in Daytona Pro Primary

Printed in Slovakia by Neografia

Acknowledgements
The publisher would like to thank the following for their kind permission to reproduce their photographs:

(Key: b-bottom c-centre l-left r-right t-top)

123RF.com: Aleksanderdn 17, Anothai Thiansawang 5, belchonock 93, Bschonewille 61, Cathy Yeulet 60, 61, Denis Rozhnovsky 88, Fabrizio Robba 38, famveldman 92, Konstantin Kalishko 90, Muriel Kerr 10, Pavel Gulea 10, Peter Zijlstra 43, Ruslan Gilmanshin 10, Sergey Novikov 88, Susan Leggett 9, Teppei Ogawa 39, Vassiliy Prikhodko 42, Wavebreak Media Ltd 93, wrangel 55, ximagination 71, yobro10 92; **Alamy Stock Photo:** Aflo Co., Ltd 73, Algirdas Grigaitis 8, Juha Jarvinen 70; **Getty Images:** Bernard Jaubert 71, bradleym 65, desifoto 69, hadynyah 26, heidijpix 71, jaroon 69, JohnnyGreig 36, Lucidio Studio Inc 65, Nick David 48, Peter Cade 93, Richard Drury 71, Tatiana Rovenskaya/EyeEm 21, 31, Wokephoto17 70; **Image Source:** Nigel Riches 47; **Pearson Education Ltd:** Gaurav Sehdev/ Mammoth Designz Studio 80, Jon Barlow 9, 19, 27, 29, 41, 51, 63, 73, 88, 89, 90, 91, 92, 93, Rafal Trubisz, Marcin Rosinski. Pearson Central Europe SP. Z.O.O. 31, Studio 8 49, Trevor Clifford 47; **Plus One:** Andy Macdonald of MiArchitects, Telly Theodore and Danella Bennett 26; **Shutterstock:** 17, 70, 88, 92, absolut 8, Aflo 26, Ahmad Ihsan 69, 69, Alex Staroseltsev 42, AlexMaster 17, Andrey Eremin 43, andrey_l 33, 53, Anna Nahabed 75, Anurak Pongpatimet 93, AP 60, austrian photographer 20, 31, Babka 48, 50, 51, ducu59us 49, Elizaveta Rozhkova 61, Gelpi JM 47, GOLFX 54, 75, GrashAlex 20, Iakov Filimonov 88, Invisible163 74, iQoncept 5, 9, jayk67 91, JiliPaper 8, John Kasawa 17, John_T 61, Kara Knight 60, Kevin Eaves 90, Kozlik 36, Lina Truman 79, Lopolo 65, Luigi Bertello 43, Macrovector 79, Maria Siubar 27, Mayabuns 20, 31, mayoyoma 33, 53, Milan Tomazin 71, Nach-Noth 70, New Africa 36, Nikuwka 16, Ohmega1982 90, Pakhnyushchy 90, REDPIXEL.PL 5, Samuel Borges Photography 47, Sara Winter 61, Sergiy Kuzmin 17, SeventyFour 36, Silvia Izquierdo/AP 38, Studio_G 79, sylv1rob1 61, taelove7 9, 16, Tatiana Bobkova 92, United Photo Studio 21, Valentyn Volkov 43, wavebreakmedia 88, windwalk 88

Cover Image: *Front:* **Alamy Stock Photo:** View Stock

All other images © Pearson Education

Illustrated by BluBlu Studios (main character artwork); A Corazon Abierto /Sylvie Poggio: p. 89; Valentina Bandera /Sylvie Poggio: pp. 19, 28, 40, 50, 62, 72; Ruth Bennett /The Bright Agency: pp. 82-87; Iryna Boiko /Sylvie Poggio: pp. 6, 12, 22, 34, 44, 56, 66; Maria Kiryakova pp. 34 (activity 1 items 2 and 3), 37 (activity 2 the man)), 40 (activity 1 items 1 and 4), 62, 66 (activity 1 items 3 and 6), 72 (items 2, 4, 5, 9); Jen Naalchigar /The Bright Agency: pp. 17 (Ex 1), 18, 29, 41; Elisa Rocchi /Beehive Illustration: pp. 78-81; Simona Rossi /Sylvie Poggio: pp. 30, 31, 53; Alan Rowe /Beehive Illustration: pp .15, 25, 37, 47, 59, 69, Pronunciation, 21 Grammar; Ana Sebastian /The Bright Agency: pp. 46, 58; Skylar White /The Bright Agency: pp .8, 16A, 49; Nuno A Viera /Beehive Illustration: pp. 15 (Ex 1), 25 (Ex 1), 37 (Ex 1), 47 (Ex 1), 59 (Ex 1), 69 (Ex 1).